THE MEMOIR OF A PASTOR:

A Journey Of Love, Forgiveness, And Repentance

"Therefore if any man be in Christ, he is a new creature: old things are passed away; behold, all things are become new."
2 Corinthians 5:17 KJV

Latina C. Campbell

Copyright © 2020 Latina C. Campbell

All rights reserved. No part of this book may be reproduced in any form or by any electronic or mechanical means, including information storage and retrieval systems, without permission in writing from the publisher, except by reviewers, who may quote brief passages in a review.

ISBN: 978-1-7354871-1-3
Printed in the United States of America

Story Corner Publishing Inc.
6024 Churchland Blvd. suite 10
Portsmouth, VA 23703
Storycornerpublishing@yahoo.com

Table of Contents

Life Purpose Plan..1
Chapter 1 The Shift Of My Life...3
Chapter 2 My "Yes" To God: My Walk Of Salvation..........6
Chapter 3 The Assignment...11
Chapter 4 The Wounds Of A "First" Lady.........................15
Chapter 5 Starting God's Ministry......................................21
Chapter 6 Answering The Call..29
Chapter 7 The Process Of Pastorship..................................36
Chapter 8 Building Character...52
Chapter 9 My Becoming Of A Pastor..................................59

Dedication

I dedicate this book to all those who are called and chosen by God that people have counted out. I pray that as you read this book a boldness shall fall upon you and the power of the Lord shall overtake you. I pray that you come out of hiding and do all that God has assigned you to do no matter what! I pray strength, healing, encouragement, and restoration over you now, in Yeshua/ Jesus name, Amen.

Husband/ Apostle, Paul Campbell Jr,

Thank you for believing in me when no one else did. Thank you for hearing and obeying God to push me into purpose when I didn't even think I could do it. Thank you for your countless prayers on my behalf and never giving up on me. We went through so much during this season of live, but I'm just glad we were able to go through these storms TOGETHER! I would not change it for anything. I love you to the moon and back!

Prayer

Dear Father/God/Yahweh,

Thank you for being all that you are to me! I honor you as ABBA, Master, The Most High God, Holy, Hosanna, Righteous, Perfect in all of your ways, and so much more! You are truly everything to me. Hallelujah!

Thank you for saving me, delivering me, healing me, restoring me, covering me, and protecting me. God please forgive me for all of my sins known and unknown in the name of Yeshua/Jesus. God I pray that this book reaches all of the people you intend for it to reach. I pray that each of them would be blessed by my testimony and that you would push them along in whatever part of the process they are in! I pray that you love on them like never before. I pray you grant them endurance, mercy, and grace to go on each day and to get through their process. I cancel the assignment of Satan right now for each of their lives in Yeshua/ Jesus name. I pray that you cover them in your blood right now and protect them from all hurt, harm, and danger. I pray you open their eyes and ear to be extra sensitive to your spirit and your Will for their lives. Please Lord give them clear instructions, direction, and interpretation for their life and destiny. I pray you build them up when they are weak and carry them when they can't take another step in the name of Yeshua/Jesus. I pray you reveal to them who you are calling them to be and give them courage to walk it out no matter what, in Yeshua/Jesus name, Amen!

Life Purpose Plan

– Love: an intense feeling of deep affection (physical action of love).

"Love is patient, love is kind. It does not envy, it does not boast, it is not proud. It does not dishonor others, it is not self-seeking, it is not easily angered, it keeps no record of wrongs. Love does not delight in evil but rejoices with the truth. It always protects, always trusts, always hopes, always perseveres. Love never fails." 1 Corinthians 13:4-8 NIV

– Forgiveness: stop feeling angry or resentful toward (someone) for an offense, flaw, or mistake.

"And forgive us our debts, as we also have forgiven our debtors. For if you forgive other people when they sin against you, your heavenly Father will also forgive you. But if you do not forgive others their sins, your Father will not forgive your sins." Matthew 6:12, 14-15 NIV

– Repentance: the action of repenting; sincere regret or remorse.

"Repent, then, and turn to God, so that your sins may be wiped out, that times of refreshing may come from the Lord," Acts 3:19 NIV

Chapter 1

Life without God seemed amazing! I partied hard often, took vacations frequently, and could get any man I wanted. I had everything this world had to offer. I had all types of men throwing themselves at my feet. They were just a phone call away. I had the money, cars, fancy clothes, nice house, jewelry, independence, etc. I was living my dream life which was to live better than I did in my childhood. I made sure of it! By any means necessary. I was living the dream life for years until I realized that something was missing. I could not put my finger on it, but I knew there was a void. The void always seemed to show up when I was alone in a quiet place. It would feel like death and sound like it was screaming at me like a loud siren every time I would settled myself. I didn't understand! I could buy everything I ever wanted and be with whoever I wanted, but that still wasn't good enough. I thought that was what life was all about, but the empty space was still there. Nothing I did was good enough when it came to filling the empty space. After a while, I began to realize money, men, or material things wasn't the answer to my problem after all.

Allow me to introduce myself. I was born and raised in Camden, New Jersey. It is a small poor town with a vibrant culture and high in crime. I was born Latina C. Thomas to Audrey Thomas and Waddy Russell Sr. My father passed away when I was twenty-one years old and it hurt like hell! I was a daddy's girl, so it took me a while to recover. This was a major turning point for my family and I because my father was the glue that held us all together. I am part of a blended family, three sisters and five brothers. I only seen my fifth brother twice right after he was born, because he was quickly adopted by another family around that time. That's another story for another day, although I do pray we would meet again. I grew up poor with no food some times, no electric half of the time, and thrift store clothes most of the time. Our house was most certainly not in the best of shape, but it was home. A piece of the house fell apart every week! My parents were barely able to stay ahead of the repairs before they just gave up. I hated the way we had to live in my childhood days, so I made a vow to myself to live better no matter what it took to achieve.

I graduated high school, started college, had a child, and ended up becoming a single mother that had to work for everything on my own. I thought I would be married, living in my own home, driving a fancy car, and enrolled in a prestigious university right after high school. Instead, I was a single mother, living in an apartment, with an okay car, and attending community college. It wasn't a bad start on my own, but I just had different expectations/plans. I wanted more out of life! I wanted to be successful on a greater scale.

Needless to say, greater success did not happen fast enough for me. I started drinking and hanging out at parties on the regular with college friends. I was the quiet type that stayed to myself, so this was a big step in my life. Then it happened, my conservative shell broke. The good girl had left the building. I was introduced to a whole new world that I honestly was not ready for, but I loved every minute of it. I became wild and willing to do anything. I felt like I only had one life to live, so why not give life my all? Literally my all! Between being a mother, working, partying, sleeping around with men and sometimes women, I didn't have any time to rest! This life style went on for some years until I found out I was pregnant with my second child. I ended up leaving that baby's father because of abuse. Now a single mother of two, I had to make some drastic life changes. I slowed all the way down on drinking and partying. I barely had the free time to do it anyway. I had to regain focus on my life and move forward full speed ahead.

Chapter 2

My money started drying up, so I had to get a second job. At my second job, I became close friends with one of my co-workers. I normally do not mix business with my personal life, but there was definitely something different about him. Once he opened up to me, he read me my whole life by way of the Holy Spirit. At that time, I did not know much about God or Jesus, and surely did not know who the Holy Spirit was at all. I was spooked out because I was lost as to how he knew so much about me and we had just formally met. My co-worker told me the Holy Spirit spoke to him about my life and I looked at him strange. I asked him if he was a psychic and then he looked back at me strange. That was the most awkward and intriguing moment of my life. I grew curious to hear more, even though it was all about me. I should already know about me, right? He said the Holy Spirit is the spirit of God and it was because of God that he knew about me. My heart skipped a beat and I dropped to my knees in shock. I could not believe that God showed up to talk to me. I began to cry so much that I could not catch my breath! I cried a supply of tears that I never knew I had! I've always wanted to know all about God. Obviously God already knew all about me, so it was only right that I got to know Him.

My co-worker looked me in the eyes and asked me if I was "saved." I looked him right back in the eyes and said I don't know. My co-worker expressed that it was better to have Jesus and not need him, rather need Jesus and not have him. So I thought about it and it made sense, but what was the point of Jesus?

Who was Jesus for real? I've heard a lot of church people talk about him during "Easter," but what really did it all mean? I wanted my own foundation of proof. They would say Jesus died for us, but How? When? Where? Why? I wanted details. I just always had so many questions. My co-worker explained to me that Jesus is the son of God, He was crucified (died) for our sins, and was resurrected by God three days later. Oddly enough, I believed that. It was never broken down to me why we need Jesus and not just God. He gave me this scripture:

> *"Jesus answered," I am the way and the truth and the life. No one comes to the Father except through me. If you really know me, you will know my father as well. From now on, you do know him and have seen him."*
> *John 14:6-7 NIV*

He told me Jesus & God was one in the same. Jesus was God in the flesh & God is spirit in Heaven. I was blown away to realize just how powerful God is! He said God had three parts, which was the Holy Trinity. It consisted of The Father, The Son, & The Holy Spirit. The Father is referred to as God. The son is Jesus, and The Holy spirit is the power/Spirit of God.

He went on to say in order to get into Heaven I had to accept salvation, which is Jesus Christ. I definitely wanted to get into Heaven, but I was nervous for some reason. I knew if I started on this path that there would be no turning back. I knew getting to know God wasn't a bad thing. In fact, that was something I always wanted to do, but I wasn't planning on doing it at this time. I wanted to run the streets, party, and drink a little longer while I could. I always thought God was for old people (especially old ladies) because that's all I seen in church. HaHaHa... Don't judge me. My co-worker began to remind me of all the times God covered me from bad things in my life and it was because He had need of me. I knew God was speaking this night because my co-worker did not know me at all. I had to make the toughest decision of my life. I thought I had to make tough decisions before, but this one was the end all be all. It was choosing between life or death. It was the decision that would dictate my life for the rest of my life.

> *"If you declare with your mouth, "Jesus is Lord," and believe in your heart that God raised him from the dead, you will be saved. For it is with your heart that you believe and are justified, and it is with your mouth that you profess your faith and are saved."*
> *Romans 10:9-10 NIV*

I decided to trust God, step out on faith, and give my life over to Him August 2016. I was confident with the decision I made and was so excited that I told everyone. I just felt like a new person. I knew something about me was different. My desires changed and even my perspective about life started to change. I stopped drinking, partying, and sleeping around with people all together. I felt a huge relief!! I didn't realize how much that weighed me down. I thought I was out trying to make my life better, but in fact, I was making my life worse.

After a week of being saved by the grace of God, I started to read the bible. I've never read it before, but now I had a desire to never put it down. I was wrapped up that much in the pages. Days later, I felt the strong need to "Fast." I did not know anything about it or how to do it, so I knew it was God pulling me to it. My best friend at the time would go to church on the regular, so I reach out to her so she could explain to me how it was done. She thought I was crazy because she never heard me speak of such things, but she started explaining. After she was done, she asked me why I wanted to know? I told her I believed God was calling me to do it, because I surely would not have thought to do it on my own. I couldn't get rid of the thought. I definitely felt crazy telling her this, but I knew I had to do it in order to clear my thoughts. She told me to take things slow so I didn't relapse or go back to my old ways, but I knew I had changed already and that wouldn't be the case. Therefore, I did not worry about that and moved full speed ahead. She told me about a "Daniels Fast," but it did not make sense to me. I had so many questions about that type of so-called "Fast." I attempted to do a 3-day Daniel's fast and it made me so frustrated after looking over a list of things I could not eat! One of the things on the list was sugar and that is in mostly all food products. After reading so many ingredient labels, I ended up not eating anything at all and just drank water so I didn't have a dry mouth.

After I made it through my three day fast, I felt refreshed and could see everything in a different light. I wanted to live right before God, so I started cutting people, places, and things out of my life that meant me no good. I even gave my body over to God and became celibate until God decided to send me a husband, if He wanted to. My thought process was, even if God did not send me a husband, I was more than happy with God being my husband. Sure I had physical needs, but God was really keeping me all the way around through the process. Yes, God was my husband because I accepted His son (Jesus Christ) into my life. When we accept salvation, we become married to God and I'm glad about it because He is perfect in all His ways. I've been through too much at this point in my life to turn back and just accept anybody, like I use to. Once the cleansing process in my life started, I knew it was overdue & much needed.

"For your Maker is your husband— the Lord Almighty is his name— the Holy One of Israel is your Redeemer; he is called the God of all the earth." Isaiah 54:5 NIV

I finally felt free! For once in my life I didn't want to drink my pain away! I didn't want to dance my pain away. I didn't want to sex my pain away. I didn't want to sleep my pain away either. The love I felt from God was like nothing I've ever felt before. I never knew I could be loved as such. God swept through my life, and suddenly I felt like I lived in a whole new world!

Chapter 3

I started going to my best friend at the time church on the regular just to get the understanding of God's word. I had already started reading the Bible, but the King James Version was a little hard to understand. I knew there just had to be an easier way. It was actually very fascinating to sit in a church and understand the word of God, when previously I would go to church and not understand a thing! This church really broke the word down for all to comprehend. My eyes and ears were really open to a new world. Things had been going on right in front of my face when I went to church in the past, but I was blind to it all for some reason. For example, back then I would walk in a church one way then leave the same exact way, feeling like I wasted my time and could've did something else. Now that my eyes were open, I go into a service where GOD IS and I leave changed more & more every time. I understand now that it's all a process. I now had to be reprogramed and cleanse of 30 years of what the world taught me. What the world or society teaches us is not the same things God want us to learn or digest. In fact, most times it's the complete opposite! The Bible declares:

> "Surely I was sinful at birth, sinful from the time my mother conceived me."
> Psalms 51:5 NIV

Anything against God is sin! I had a mind-blowing experience each day as I learned the new ways of life that pleased God.

As I allowed God to order my steps, He removed me from the only church I was comfortable at and lead me to a church where my husband found me! Yes, you read correctly. A husband! I was wondering what God had up His sleeve for me, then out of nowhere it was revealed to me. As I stated before, what society recommends or place as the norm and what God requires are two different things. My husband-to-be was just installed as a pastor and God revealed to me that he was the gift that He prepared for me. I was shocked because I would have never thought I would be married to a pastor, especially since I just got saved and started going to church faithfully. I felt like God had prepared a pastor for me to make sure I would not turn back to my old ways. Little did I know, it was because God had need of me on a much bigger scale! God designed me to be a curse breaker, so although I felt like I wasn't worthy to marry a pastor and people even said I wasn't good enough for him, God graced me and wanted to use me to free him from the curse that he was under. So we got married December 2016. God began to reveal details of the curse. My husband was entangled by lies, manipulation, religion, control, lust, witchcraft, and sexual perversion. Of course, I did not know all of this in the beginning, or I would've ran far, far away! It wasn't until we were married that these things were revealed to me and it was Hell trying to stand firm in my assignment, and in my marriage at the same time! I knew nothing about these spirits nor how to break them off of my husband. All I knew was that it was frustrating to see it all running rapid in my presence! I began to pull on God for answers like never before.

I thought God was paying me back for the unsaved life He pulled me from. Or maybe it wasn't really God that told me to marry "This" man. I hated everything about my marriage during this beginning phase of the assignment. People say this is suppose to be the best part of marriage, but instead I wanted a divorce every other day!!!! The way I was beat down, stripped, and talked about, I truly felt like Jesus on the cross every single day! The abuse was so great I felt like I was going crazy. I was abused in every way except physically, but the stress levels that I endured was enough physical abuse to my body to last a lifetime. All I wanted to know was when will it end. The process that is. I was beat down by just about everyone. People I thought would be happy for me, wasn't! So many turned away from me. So many talked about me like a dog, family included! In fact, our families were the first in line! So many lies, envy, jealousy, hatred, and scandals! I thought I would experience some relief in "church," boy was I wrong. "Church" was the first place I felt lifeless, stuck, and depressed all the more, not knowing the curses originated there. They were the ones trying to change my husband's mind about me because they wanted him to remain stuck with them in darkness, just like crabs in a barrel. They felt they had the upper hand because they were there first, but that's not how God's order work. They tried to push me to the back because I was just a new comer on the scene and we all know how the new comer gets treated. The person "in charge" or the "leader of the pack" don't want the new person taking their spotlight, so they treat them like trash so that no one else would like them and all attention would remain on them.

I've been through this too many times in life, so it really didn't phase me. I didn't care about being liked or accepted, but what I didn't like was my husband siding with them instead of covering me as his wife. God began to show me that this was the power of the demonic force or demonic spirits that needed to be broken off of him. I could only remember asking God, WHY

ME??? Why did I have to be the one chosen for this assignment and marriage?? Why couldn't God Himself just do it for my husband? God shared with me that He gave us the power to do as His son Jesus Christ did and one of those things were to cast out or drive out demons.

I started rethinking everything! If it wasn't for the vow I made with GOD even before my husband was a thought, I would've cut everybody out of my life, including my husband!!! When I say everyone, that's just what I meant! I would've gotten my kids and moved to a place no one could find us. Getting married was the second big step I took during my process of getting closer to God. The first was saying "Yes" to salvation, His will, and becoming celibate! These two steps were big because they both involved denying myself and what I wanted to do! With celibacy, I could no longer satisfy myself with the lust of the world. My marriage forced me to walk in love and to deny the ways of my flesh. No longer could I act out and leave when I felt some type of way. I had to have patience and walk in love and kindness even when I didn't want to.

Not only did I have to walk in love in my marriage, but I had to do this with everyone!! That was even harder because once I started changing my ways to the ways of God, people took my meekness and humbleness for weakness! It made my pride jump out of the box a number of times until I got tired of the consequences from God. Pride had to go. Forget what the people thought or how they felt, I was not trying to get in trouble with God any longer. I was making my relationship with God look bad to everyone that saw Him through me every time I allowed pride to take over. I had let God down too many times and I did not like that feeling. God definitely taught me better, but I failed to do better at times. I had to make a change and fast!

Chapter 4

I began to get myself together and stood by husband's side for better and for worse, and also in ministry. It hurt, but I had an assignment to do. Living life now as the pastor's wife was definitely something new to me because I didn't realize all the made up rules the "church" had placed on the ministry leaders wives.

The "church" told me I had to dress a certain way, sit a certain way, and act a certain way. They felt I had to be saved a certain period of time before I could wavy or speak to the members. The church told me unless I was born and raised in the church and came from a long family line of preachers, I had no right to marry a preacher. I was the outcast! The "church" wanted my husband all for themselves and hated the fact that I showed up and took my place by his side. This was no easy task by any means, but I knew only I could fill the position and accomplish what the others did not have grace to do.

Doing anything in God's Will is no easy task because of the warfare you have to face. My marriage was the first thing I had to give back to God because the attacks were so great! At this point, only God could work it out. My marriage wasn't completely horrible. My husband just welcomed everyone into our marriage like it was a talk show and chaos was breaking out at all sides. All of the people he welcomed did not want us married in the first place. They actually was taking bets to see how long we lasted in marriage. They didn't think we had what it took and certainly didn't think God called us to be together. Too many people were trying to tear us apart. They would try to pull me one way and pull my husband another way. They were planting discord and lies into our marriage so we could fight each other and split up. We almost spilt a few times because of the people! People really didn't want us happy together because they were lonely, miserable, or didn't understand how God could put us together. Most of them desired marriage for years with no ring in sight or they were in a relationship, but it was struggling so they surely didn't want to see us happy.

This was definitely a big factor that was ruining our marriage. I just couldn't do anything else on my part, but pray. I felt so frustrated, alone, and thought about divorce every single day. I knew my husband didn't really realize what he was doing by welcoming everyone because he is the type that think everyone comes with good intentions. I, on the other hand trust NO man until God gives the approval. I can see right through the mask people wear! I guess this is why some people really don't like me because they can't get over on me. They will slither like a snake to my husband instead though. We had so many arguments about this with no change in sight. Then I realized my husband did not trust my judgement because the people already got into his ears! I knew my husband loved me, but it was overshadowed by everything that was going on. I just wanted out of my marriage. Maybe that would've put an end to the warfare. What God showed me was that the enemy wanted me dead no matter if I was married or not because I was a threat to his agenda. The enemy hated that I accepted salvation and that I could see things for what they really were. Satan likes to stay hidden so he could ruin people's lives behind the scenes while we think the attacks are coming from somewhere else. When God's hand is upon you, no demon of Hell can interfere with God's plan for your life. God stepped in like a rushing wind and took over in my marriage. He even showed me another level of love in Him. The love I experience from God can not be compared to anything in my life. If it had not been for the love of God, this is where my story would've ended. It still amazes me that God loves anyone who accepts Him! Being a pastor's wife in a God ordained Kingdom marriage, you definitely need God there for you every step of the way. God fights your battles for you and He protects you no matter what. God being by my side and loving me is something sacred to me. It is what got me through the storms of life. I wouldn't trade it for anything in the world!

My husband started loving me better and even began to put me first, how it should be, instead of listening to the people! I started to have more patience with him and allowed God to show me how to be his wife instead of just wanting to leave. We finally got to a place in our marriage that we closed the doors on everyone and everything. No one should come between husband and wife, but GOD!!! If they wasn't God, they had to goooooo!!!! We had to take a stand and be there for each other no matter who didn't like it! WE have a marriage and family to protect and could not do that always fighting each other because of what the people sent our way. Our Marriage and Our Kids had to be first!!! Everything else could wait, and if it's not sent from God we didn't even acknowledge it. God now stands, rest, and rules in the middle of our marriage! No matter what person, place, or thing tries to separate the union that God brought together, it won't work. In fact, I feel sorry for all of those who are still trying to intervene in our marriage. God lives in this marriage and He sees all.

Now back to operating in ministry as a "first lady" or shall I say the pastor's wife. The way "church" people treat a pastor's wife is disrespectful, cruel, and nasty! The way churches operate these days are different from what I saw when I was younger attending church with my grandmother. Maybe they were just more discreet with the mess they did then versus now. Don't get me wrong, some churches carry the authentic presence of God and operate in love, but most… Well you get my point. I pray they get delivered and fast before they run across the wrong person to play with!

Holding the pastor's wife title does have it's "pro's" and "con's" as I have shared some "con's" with you already. I definitely have a long list of con's as a matter of fact and I'm still trying to figure out more than two "pro's." Hmmmmm.... let me think and get back to you. For starters, I hate being called "first lady!" The term makes no sense to a sane person and most importantly it's not a biblical term. If believers of Christ follow the Bible, why are we using terms that isn't according to the scriptures?? If there is a First lady, who is the Second and the third lady?? I'm just saying. Something to think about, right??

Second, it's almost like the "church" code is that the pastor's wife should never speak or even be seen! It's like they just want her to disappear. People believe "church" is a man's world and women just live to serve. The devil is a liar and so are all those that believe such foolishness. Now do not get me wrong because we are all, or should be servants of the Lord. People will see my husband and I together and never even acknowledge me. It's like the pastor's wife is invisible, or we don't matter to the people. We are just supposed to sit pretty and smile just in case someone sees us by accident. Third, almost everyone in the church wishes they were with my husband just because he is a pastor. Since when did that become the norm? I only became a pastor's wife because God said so, or I would've definitely ran the other way and chose someone else! Anybody else!

In the "church" world lust and sexual perversion is so high that you literally have to get approval from God Himself before even entering inside of a building. You can not go to every church because your life is at hand. Our natural lives and the spiritual world is connected hand and hand. If things happen in the spiritual world concerning your life, it will manifest in your natural life as well. Demonic strongholds that dwell in the churches are waiting to connect to a weak vessel in the natural. A couple of demonic strongholds are fornication, adultery, lust, and sexual perversion that spread like wildfire. Almost everyone is sleeping with everyone these days. Adultery and formication is out of control and secret same sex relationships go on like it's nothing! Men and women alike. I've witnessed men and women flirting with my husband right in front of my face. My husband even revealed to me, after a disturbing dream I had, that another married male pastor sent him a picture of his private area to his social media inbox right after we met the man at a service for the first time! The disrespect! I wanted to kill the man. I really wanted to show up to that pastor's church and show his wife and members what he sent my husband! That's just one situation, but I could go on and on. Being mature is hard when you don't want to be, but I know it's for the better. God can handle them better than I can and I know that for a Fact!

I was raised in the hood, and where I'm from we fought right then and there if someone disrespected us, let alone our relationship! It always took everything inside of me to handle those situations in a mature and graceful manner. Not only was I representing my husband, but most importantly I was representing

God! I knew God was grooming me to be above all the mess I've witnessed in my life, including church and the streets. God was maturing the fruits on the inside of me and I couldn't go backwards unless I wanted to prolong my process! I hated my process, but I was thankful for it because it was making me a better person. Remember, love should be the main root you plant in God's ministry and allow God to do the rest. He is the fair and just Judge and He will vindicate on our behalf.

> *"The Lord will vindicate his people and relent concerning his servants when he sees their strength is gone and no one is left, slave or free."*
> *Deuteronomy 32:36 NIV*

I've even heard someone announce they had throat cancer after putting their mouth on me as a wife and as a mother. I remember wanting to square up with them, but God grabbed hold of me to calm down so He could take care of the situation. When you are in the right, God will rise up on your behalf. All you do is just stand. Knowing this helps me to get through every messy situation that comes my way.

Chapter 5

Church became a place I really dreaded to go! I began to hate everything about it even the day we went, Sunday! I did not like to see Sundays because it was the day of the week that I had to put up with the most mess. Most churches made me sick just to step foot in the front door and I haven't been to that many churches. I've probably witnessed about seven or eight, and that was too many for me. So much competition, so many lies, gossip, scandals, and people just plainly out of order. There were no souls saved, no deliverance, nor any lives changed. I began to question if God was even there at all. I just figured that the "church" people were bored, lonely, and did not want to stay home, so they went to church. They went to church to get in other people's business so they would have something to talk about all week. The pastor's wife stood no chance in this circus if she was not strong! Going to church for God was the last thing the people did. I hated what I was witnessing.

I ended up taking some time away from the club called "church" just to spend some alone time with God. Sometimes it was hard to hear Him through all of the "church" noise, or shall I say chatter in the church building. They ran their mouths about everything and everyone. I needed a break! Enough was enough, so I took a break! I wanted to continue to be in right standing with God, so I couldn't react how I really wanted. I definitely wanted to curse people out and lay hands on them!

Oh they tempted and tested me, but I already seen their plan ahead of time! They wanted me to give them something to talk about and I wasn't about to do that. I had to stay the course.

During my time alone with God, He showed me that my husband and I were to start our own ministry. I almost fell to the floor! I had to ask God to show me again because I just had to be confused or mistaken! I was in disbelief and in total shock! I just walked away from the church and not only is He saying to go back, but to start one of our own??? What?? Why?? I wanted to curse in that moment, but I had to get myself together because I was talking to God. The Holy Creator that could take my life in the blink of an eye, so I had to relax. I did NOT want to get involved with starting a ministry. I just wasn't in the mood to deal with people like the ones I just walked away from.

I didn't know anything about starting a ministry and was not interested in knowing anything either! I'm sure my husband didn't know how to start one either even though he was born and raised in the church and his mother was a preacher too. It's definitely more than just holding a microphone on a Sunday morning inside of a building! It's more than praying for someone or announcing an altar call. I was nervous and afraid of the unknown, but I prayed that our ministry would not look like anything we have ever seen!! I would make sure of that. That was probably the only part that brought me comfort. I eventually told my husband and he looked at me crazy. Come to find out God had already revealed this to him and he just didn't want to say anything to me about it. He knew if he said something to me about it, he would have had to put things into action. He also knew I was ready to transition to another ministry altogether, I just wasn't thinking to start our own! My husband didn't say anything because he was comfortable where he was under his mother's covering. It was time to obey God and get out of our thoughts, feeling, and comfortability.

One thing I do know is that God will put us in uncomfortable situations to push us to grow. God did just that no matter who liked it or not. We surely did not want to do it for different reasons, but God's Word and Will shall always prevail. We brought it up to our leader at the time only to be disapproved. She did not believe it was God's will or timing for our life, so we went back to God and He instructed us to continue forward anyway. We stepped out and started our own ministry with the help of a couple of unexpected people, but we knew they were God sent. We were negatively talked about, persecuted, and hated for doing what God told us to do and when He told us to do it. We didn't care, nor were we upset because we understood the life of Jesus and these things happened to Him as well. It was tough not having the support of family, the church, and so-called friends, but God gave us the strength and resources to do His Will for our lives! So many people tried to tell us what wasn't God's Will for our lives, but could never tell us what "was" His Will concerning our lives! Better yet, they couldn't tell us what God's Will was for their own lives because they were too busy checking for us that they did not even know. The "know-it-alls" of the "church" is what I called them, but they really didn't know anything. I was even wondering if they knew God for real. This was always funny to me, when it didn't get on my nerves that is.

Building a ministry from the ground up with the guidance of God's Holy Spirit was like nothing I ever imagined. It showed me the ministry side of "church" and I fell in love from that moment. It was hard and tedious work, but it was worth it to see God move firsthand. I've seen a lot of entertaining and embarrassing shows in the "church," but to see the real ministry of Jesus Christ come alive in our ministry was amazing to witness. Of course, I'm sure the ministry of Jesus was alive in other ministries, I just haven't run across many. We made sure the love of God was truly displayed in all that we did and towards all that we encountered. This was a heavy mandate, but with God all things are possible.

Now fighting two streams of warfare made me exhausted. The stream of demons that came with the pastor's wife title and the stream that came with founding a ministry was intense! You would think the people in the church treated people better than the worldly people because the church people allegedly have Jesus Christ as a role model, right? Surely not all do! Jesus Christ is love and mercy, so they should have that too. Yes, Jesus flipped over a table or two because of the disrespect the people did in His Father's house, but He showed us how love and mercy is suppose to be put into action overall. He could've just killed everyone who wronged Him, but He didn't. I know I wanted to flip over a table or two over time attending church, but I had to display love and mercy and allow God to handle the rest.

> *"Whoever claims to love God yet hates a brother or sister is a liar. For whoever does not love their brother and sister, whom they have seen, cannot love God, whom they have not seen. And he has given us this command: Anyone who loves God must also love their brother and sister."*
>
> *1 John 4:20-21 NIV*

True believers should have the love of God for each other. God commands us to love one another, but it seems like it's more love in the streets where people die everyday than in the church. After a couple of weeks away from the church scene,

I had to remember our purpose as believers is to advance the Kingdom of God by doing ministry, not "church." We are the CHURCH that Jesus Christ is coming back for. We have to live holy and blameless and we can't do that without following the command of loving one another.

> *"and to present her to himself as a radiant church, without stain or wrinkle or any other blemish, but holy and blameless."*
> *Ephesians 5:27 NIV*

We get so caught up thinking the church building is the end all be all. When in fact it's just a building were believers gather to learn God's Word and to get strengthened enough to go out and share with others what they learned. The church building is also one of many places a unbeliever could go to get "saved" and gain a deeper understanding of God, Jesus, and The Holy Spirit. Then, they are to go out to the world and lead others to Jesus Christ by spreading the good news of His Gospel and sharing their testimony. Now that's ministry! Going out to those who do not know Jesus and winning souls is the purpose of it all. I had to realize that it wasn't about me or anyone else for that matter. It was all about glorifying God. I felt convicted in that moment, so I repented and return to the "church." I couldn't allow people, places, or things to detour me from doing ministry anymore. I had been through too much already to give up now. My husband and I were told we couldn't do ministry because we wasn't old enough, didn't know God long enough, couldn't be trusted to do ministry alone, or didn't have enough money stored up in the bank. We were also told we couldn't do ministry because we would sometimes argue with each other. Apparently, they thought my husband and I were never suppose to argue or disagree (when most of the arguments were because of those people in the first place) with each other in order to do ministry together. If that was the case, all ministries would and should be shut down immediately! My husband and I continued to follow God.

Despite what everyone else said, did, and/or thought, God had to be first in our lives. We put so many others first in the past, but now we had to do it the right way with God first. Going forward with the ministry God birthed through us, my husband and I faced a lot of spiritual warfare. Our marriage was the first to be under great attack! One thing I do know is when you are on the right path, Satan wants you to abort the mission so he sets traps hoping that you will fall. We had given GOD our "yes" already, so we had to continue to push and make good of it. Our process for the ministry had begun and we started losing things one by one. We had to leave our jobs and go with the vision God gave us to start businesses that we didn't know where the finances were coming from for start-up cost.

We had to leave our house and even had to split up our two children at the time so they could stay with their other dads (I brought two children by two other men into the marriage) because we did not know what was next as far as living arrangements. I was stressed all the more because I did not want our oldest kids going with their other dads. They was not steady and consistent in the kids lives, nor did the kids want to go. I knew the process would not be forever, but I just couldn't wrap my mind around this part. I had to leave my/our children behind! I had never been without them for more than a couple of days at a time, so this part of the process alone almost killed me inside! I really felt like a part of me died when we drove away from each of them. I'm sure my husband was hurt too because he had a relationship with them, but it was different for me. Before I got married, it was only us. The kids was what got me through bad days. We were inseparable until this point! Oh the tears I cried this day! Our third child was due to be born really soon and that stressed us out even more! We were just following God's instructions to Go! We stepped out on faith with no where to go and my spiritual dad asked my husband and I to join him that same day for Sunday service. We were not in the mood for service. We were looking for God to speak on our situation at hand.

All we were worried about was where we were going to sleep that night, but God told us to go to the service. My spiritual dad did not know what was really going on with us, so we knew he was lead by God to invite us to his service. We went to the service and God definitely surprised us!!!! God already instructed another pastor there to take us in his home until He transitioned us to the next place. We were relieved that was didn't have to sleep in the car. We got to the house and it surely wasn't we expected, but we had to tough it out until God moved us. We really missed being in our own house already. A couple weeks later, we went to a prenatal appointment and I was rushed to the hospital because my sac had ruptured at 29 weeks. They feared that the baby would be born then and it was a little too soon. I ended up staying in the hospital for five weeks straight with my husband by my side until the baby was born. That was the longest most depressing five weeks of my life! I thought it would never be over. I never knew I could meet so many doctors in that short period of time. Our son was born November 15, 2017 and I never knew I could feel an explosion of joy and nervousness at the same time. Our son ended up having to stay in the NICU for a month because his breathing was not up to standard. Between being at the hospital every day and still trying to find balance with seeing our other children, I think I cried and prayed myself to sleep every single day. My husband and I was so exhausted during this period of time that we skipped eating plenty of times. When our son was finally released from the hospital we were so excited, but we did not want to bring him where we were living at the time. We just felt it wasn't a place for children, especially a newborn and I'm going to leave it at that! We had no other choice in the matter, so we had to do what we had to do. We hated it, but we could not take our eyes off of God no matter what.

Chapter 6

As my husband and I continued to do ministry, the gifts on the inside of me began to awaken. I've always wanted to know my purpose in life, but never knew who to get the answers from until I accepted salvation (Jesus Christ). God had all of the answers all along and He was waiting on me to ask Him for them. For once in my life I felt confident with asking questions because I knew I would get an answer from The All Knowing. I began to ask God every question that I could think of and questions that I always wanted to know the answers to all my life. I noticed that the answers did not come immediately, but when most of them were released, it was in my dreams. I would find it weird that when I prayed, I would have dreams pertaining to my prayers. At first, I thought I was going crazy until I realized that God speaks through dreams and visions as well. I began to research the ways God could speak, and concluded that God can speak through anyone or anything because He is God and has the power to do whatever He wants!

My dreams started to become so intense that I felt as if I lived in two different worlds. I began writing down my dreams and saw them happen in real life before my own eyes. It was scary because some were good, but others were bad. Seeing manifestation would just help me to see that I was closer to God than I thought. I was honored to see secret things that was on God's mind. Some dreams would be about me, people around me, or even strangers. For some reason God trusted me with knowing certain things and I loved Him even the more for it. I even began to hear the voice of God in my dreams. I never knew that was possible, but with God All things are possible!

God began to show me who He created me to be beyond being His daughter, the wife of a pastor, a mother, and a entrepreneur. He revealed to me that I was a Pastor/shepherd of His people as well. I cried out with so many mixed emotions. At first, I wanted to ignore it. Second thought, I was scared. Third, I was shocked and honored at the the same time. I repeated it to myself every day, but it still was not fully registering in my mind. I thought it took a lot of religious process to be a pastor. I thought I had to serve and sit under a well known leader or one that had lots of years experience since I was newly saved. "I" didn't think I was ready and I'm sure "the people" would've looked at me crazy and thought the same thing. But if God say a thing, it doesn't matter what "I" or "the people" think or say. God will have His way no matter what.

So many people tried to stop the purpose and process God had for my life. I even tried to stop it by giving up even before I started. I heard the naysayers in my head before I even shared it with anyone. I started feeling unworthy of the calling and I laid it to the side. Shortly after, my husband (and pastor) came to me with the Word of The Lord because he is a Prophet as well and could hear the voice of God. He said God showed him in a dream that I was fighting with a female pastor. Then God revealed that I was fighting with the calling of a pastor, not the actual pastor lady. In that moment I understood that God still wanted what He wanted and He was waiting for me to accept. I still was not open to accepting it just yet. I just felt like I needed more time. I did not want to mess up anything and run the sheep (His people) away like I've seen in so many other ministries. Shoot, I was a sheep that ran away because of a leader. I knew it was a big responsibility because people's lives would be in my hands and their blood would be on my hands if I messed up.

I just didn't want people dying and going to hell because of me. I wanted to be right before I could lead others. I've seen too much in the short time of sitting under ministries and even visiting a few. I did not want to be like anything or anyone I ever saw. Yes, they had their blameless moments, but for the most part no one was being changed before they left the services. I had to ask God, why?? Then I seen that the leaders were all messed up as well. The people would scream, shout, fall out on the floor, then would attend the following service with the same demons. Every week would just be a cycle or routine of the same thing. I began to ask myself what happened?? Was this all just a show? Did the people get delivered and just walked right back into sin after they left church? I know when I got truly delivered, I had no desire to go back. So was this the fault of the leader or the people? I feel like if the leaders are following God and allowing God to have His way in the service, lives should be changed and they remain that way.

My life was changed as a result of God coming into my life right at my job, so why isn't that happening for others in "church?" At some point, I blame leadership, but I guess it could be the people too. If change is not happening at the top (leadership), it will never pour down to anyone else in the ministry. I knew I had issues I needed to give to God so He could change me even more. I wanted to be in order before I stepped out to lead others. Whatever the leader deals with, most times the following (members) ends up dealing with the same thing.

I wanted to spare my following from anger, depression, resentment, bitterness, insecurities, doubt, worry, and fear. That's what I was dealing with all at once.

I was going through all of these emotions that took over my mind each and every day. After going from being stable enough with everything to ending up homeless with nothing, my mind was all over the place! I felt like some days I could not get a hold of all that was happening in my life. Other days I wanted to just go to Heaven so I could be in peace. I wanted to be out of pain and misery. How was I going to lead people in this shape? Some people can, but I just couldn't. Come to find out that as God was breaking me, I was able to minister and reach people I would have never thought I could reach.

I didn't realize that everywhere I went I was sent to minister. I did not notice how I've been doing ministry all along. I began to research what a pastor was and what the job description entailed. All this time I was running from something I was doing already. I was so foolish. I had allowed the enemy to toy with my mind having me to think pastoring was something I was not equipped to do. Just know if God mandated it, He will equip you for it as well. I began to ask the Holy Spirit to train me so I could be in alignment with the Word of God. I read and studied, but I just had a desire to learn more first.

One night scrolling through social media on my phone an ad appeared advertising a ministry. Within the ad, the ministry was looking for women to join them in ministering to other women in prison. I scrolled pass it that night then seen the same ad again the following night! I knew it was for me to attend, but I was nervous. I messaged the ministry hoping no one would respond, but to my surprise they responded right back with information. I attended the orientation and was approved to join the group to minister. It happened so fast that I was still in disbelief.

I have been to a prison once in my life to visit someone's relative that I was dating at that time, and I couldn't stand it. I said I would never go back! I hated the procedure of it all. I even hated the atmosphere! It was so depressing. I understood that the people were depressed because their freedom was gone, but I just didn't want any parts of it. I thanked God every day after that for not allowing me to go to jail. In my past, I was a hot head and could go from zero to a thousand in a matter of seconds if someone disrespected me. Anger still grabs a hold of me every now and then, but nothing like it use to. Praise God!!!!

I received the date we were to go to the prison to minister during orientation and I seen a familiar face among the group. This calmed my nerves a little, although I didn't have a connection with her or knew her like that. I knew of her through my husband. The day quickly arrived to go to the prison and our car had been repossessed by then, so I had to figure out how I was going to get there. I asked the familiar face and she agreed but she was running late that day, so she sent her best friend that was to minister at the prison that day as well to pick me up instead. Her best friend was nice, warm, and welcoming. I saw her in the orientation class too, but I did not speak. I pretty much stayed to myself. Her best friend began to open up and tell me things about herself and how she felt about ministering at the prison. She was a pastor and she was nervous too.

I was shocked because I figured it came natural for people who were already pastoring. She got comfortable with me and then began to pour out what God gave her for me. My mouth fell open in amazement because I was not ready for all that God wanted to say in that moment through her. A undercover prophet! God had me on the chopping block and was ready for me to accept my calling without anymore delay. God did not want to hear any more excuses from me about receiving the title of a pastor. God let me know that our ministry was out of order until I stepped up to co-pastor along side of my husband. He wanted me to know that I was more than just the pastor's wife. Tears began to flow down my face because I hated seeing people, places, and things out of order. God gifted me to see when things were in and out of order, but little did I know I was out of order! A while back, I asked God why was our ministry at a stand-still if this was what He said to do? I thought it was because the people were right about us starting "prematurely," or the word curses our previous covering spoke over us and our ministry had taken root. It was confusing because we knew we heard God tell us to do it and when to go, but the progress was not adding up! Nothing looked like what He said. Little did I know it was because of me. I was involved in the hold up of our ministry because I doubted myself and listened to the people. I figured since they definitely didn't accept me as the pastor's wife, they surely would not accept me as a pastor!

God wanted me to know I was qualified because HE does the qualifying. After that encounter during the ride to the prison, I could not deny that I was called to pastor for a time such as this anymore. She was a stranger that did not know anything about me or my life, so I knew it was God because He knows me. I got to the prison and the familiar face greeted us and asked me about the ride there and I did not have any words for her. I was just in awe with God. I went forward with ministering to my assigned person at the prison and He used me to the point that my assigned person and I were sitting at the table in tears. In that moment, I knew without doubt that God could use anyone because not only did I minister to her, but she was ministering to me in return. This was definitely a day I would never forget.

It was time for me to line up, so I did without any more procrastination. I accepted the call God placed on my life. I got home and could not wait to tell my husband all about my day. Before I was even done telling him the word that was released to me, God gave him a date to install me as pastor! My husband gave me the date and my heart dropped. The date was a few months away and there was no turning back now.

Chapter 7

Once I accepted the calling to pastor, I was ready for the breakthrough to happen in our ministry. I figured once the breakthrough happened in our ministry, breakthrough would happen in the rest of our lives as well. My God, I was wrong! There was a breaking, but not the one I was expecting. I believe once I said, "yes" to the calling, Hell started breaking out everywhere around us. The next part of process was at hand and I surely did not know what to expect. We were already homeless living with someone else for some months now and I thought things could not get any worse until God told us to pack and leave from there. So we went on the exact date God gave us. We were happy about the release and nervous because we did not get instructions on where to go next. We had my 401k available to us since God told me to quit my job, but it was not that much and it was all we had. We went and brought a used cheap truck so we could get around again without having to rely on other people. I thought to myself, "God told us to leave our jobs, leave our home, and take nothing with us but what we could carry. He sent us to live with a perfect stranger for a short while, and now He tells us to leave this house with no known destination?" We were stressed, but had to keep trusting God. We could not turn back now because we were already out in the deep of things and nowhere to turn back to. We started packing what we could again and had to throw away even more stuff this time because we definitely had no room for it all. If it could not fit in the trunk of our vehicle, it went to the trash.

We went to motel after motel depending on prices because some nights were cheaper than others certain places. We tried our best to stretch the money hoping that God would speak quickly, but weeks went by and still no Word. Our money was getting low and we began to worry. Living in a motel is really expensive! A couple of months went by and we exhausted all of our money on living expenses, food, laundry, and gas for the car! No one would or even could help or take us in. God was closing doors on us so we couldn't seek help on our own. The help had to come from Him only. A couple people volunteered to take us in for a short period of time, but they did not want to make room for us all. They only wanted to accept me and I had to leave my husband or they only wanted to accept my husband and he had to leave me behind. We was not about to allow the enemy back into our marriage, our oneness! We finally got to a place that we were on the same page and we were not risking that for anyone! We did not want to go to the shelter because they would have separated me and the kids from my husband. They did not have family shelters that included the father/husband too! They only had space for women and children in one building and the men were put in a separate building somewhere else. We definitely were not comfortable with this arrangement either, separating and living amongst complete strangers! My husband and I agreed that no matter what, we would weather this storm together.

We really had nowhere else to go and could not believe God was still silent with us. The day was slipping away and we still didn't have a place to sleep for the night. We decided to take our youngest child to the beach so we could clear our minds from worry. Praying all the way, we were hoping God would speak. After enjoying as much time at the beach as we could before it got too dark, God was still silent!

My husband, baby son, and I ended up sleeping in our vehicle for the first time. We figured we would shield our oldest two girls from experiencing this, so we let them stay with their other dads a little while longer. We didn't have anywhere stable to live and barely had money for food! Before we knew it, one day turned into two, then a month had passed us by and we were still sleeping in the car. We began to doubt we heard from God. What is there to do in life after you start to doubt GOD??? We felt God had left us, but for some reason we couldn't give up nor stop praying. We wanted answers and needed them fast because we just couldn't stomach sleeping in the car another night! I hated the uncertainty of it all!! I wanted answers and God was silent. God showed us the ending of our process and it was worth going through for, but we definitely did not know what the beginning and middle had in store for us! I might've ran away. It hurt like Hell, I can definitely tell you that. I lost count of how many times I broke down crying and I'm not a big crier, so this broke me in more ways than I could ever imagine. We endured with pain and suffering for God's glory for sure. No one can tell us otherwise.

> "Then Jesus said to his disciples, "Whoever wants to be my disciple must deny themselves and take up their cross and follow me."
> Matthew 16:24 NIV

> "In the same way, those of you who do not give up everything you have cannot be my disciples."
> Luke 14:33 NIV

> *"If we suffer, we shall also reign with him: if we deny him, he also will deny us:"*
> 2 Timothy 2:12 KJV

We slept in the car for some time. I really lost count of the number of weeks because it was just too much trauma to store in my mind. I do know it was over a month. In the dead of summer with a baby in the truck, we barely had money to keep gas in the tank so we could turn the air conditioner on. We felt like we were in Hell or the furnace at least. I never realized how hot and humid the summertime was in July. I guess because I never really stayed outside too much during the day in the summer unless I was in air conditioner. We went through so much all for the glory of God. I felt like I was loosing my mind every day. I couldn't understand why our process was so hard. We went through a long period homelessness, no money, businesses dried up, and multiple miscarriages!! Just like Peter, we took our eyes off God when things started getting really crazy and we started to sink!

> *"'Lord, if it's you," Peter replied, "tell me to come to you on the water." "Come," he said. Then Peter got down out of the boat, walked on the water and came toward Jesus. But when he saw the wind, he was afraid and, beginning to sink, cried out, "Lord, save me!" Immediately Jesus reached out his hand and caught him. "You of little faith," he said, "why did you doubt?"'*
> Matthew 14:28-31 NIV

I thank God for sending His son to be our savior. Jesus to the rescue!! If it wasn't for Him, we would've surely died in the wilderness. Going through all of these things just to do the ministry of Jesus in a greater capacity, definitely increase our prayer life. We thought we had a prayer life before, but some days we ended up praying all day and night. God wanted us to totally depend on Him and trust Him with our whole heart! He did not want anyone to get the glory out of what He was going to do for us and with us.

The date for me to be installed as a pastor was quickly approaching and the people we had set in place to assist started reaching out for details. At this point, I did not care about my installment service at all! I hated life and everything about it. I really just wanted to die. I needed peace in my mind and could not find it. All I wanted was stability for me and my family. I wanted a place to call home again. I couldn't get over the fact that we were homeless sleeping in the car and God still wanted us to push forward. I cried out to God every day asking, WHY???? What did we do wrong? Were we in the Permissive Will instead of God's Perfect Will? The Permissive Will is sin! I was certain that this was a punishment the way our lives were going. The only thing God gave me in return was, "this process is to trust Me and only Me." God truly made it so my family and I did not and could not depend on anyone else even if we wanted to. God even cut off all outside connection and took us into a isolated wilderness. We could no longer be upset with all those that didn't help us because as we knew God made it that way.

God began to take us to the story of Job in the Bible and told us that we have been considered! I was torn because I didn't know if I should be honored or upset. If you know anything about the story of Job, God allowed Satan to take everything away from him, even his children just to prove to Satan that Job would maintain his integrity to God no matter what he loss. But at the end of that story, God gave Job back double of what he loss for passing the test! So again, I don't know if I was more honored or upset. I think I was a little of both. Job went through

Hell before it got better. He even had the people closest to him mock his situation and tell him he was out of the Perfect Will of God because of sin. They were saying that was the reason he lost everything, not that he was considered by God. My family and I were going through the same exact attack from the people close to us. So I knew God was forewarning us.

Everyone that knew a glimpse of what we were going through said we were in sin and out of the Perfect Will of God concerning our life. They mocked us and our situation. They refused to help us even when they said God sent them to help! But they just wanted to hear more of the details of our story so they could have more to talk about. During this time, God was shaping me to be quiet and to allow Him to fight the battles, or shall I say His battles that came our way. God was exposing everyone's true character around us. All those who claimed to have a relationship with God, love God, and walked Holy were all liars and hypocrites! They were users, abusers, misleaders, and manipulators. They were lychees that only wanted to take advantage and never wanted to give a helping hand unless God forced their back up against the wall. It sure wasn't out of the kindness of their heart. Some even admitted that they didn't want to help even though God said! It took for us to be without to see them all for who they truly were. There were contaminated people who needed God to work on their heart and fill them with love again. I, on the other hand, saw a number of them for who they really were before we lost everything, but our situation just made them more bold! My husband finally started seeing people in light of who they truly were.

Our own mothers were first in line to try and tear us to shreds mentally, emotionally, and spiritually. We couldn't believe it because we thought they were suppose to be the most supportive, sense we were their biggest supporters for the longest! Just know when God put something together and has His hand on it, no one can separate it or stop it. God was going to make sure His Will would continue on no matter who didn't like it. I know we definitely did not like the process and we begged God to make it stop, but we had to be obedient and make it to the finish line. Our purpose depended on it. Our lives depended on it. Our children depended on it. My husband and I both went through homelessness with our parents when we were younger, so I believe God used that for our adult process because we seen how to make it through or maybe our parents did not complete a task, so it fell on us to complete. We definitely did not choose to be homeless like so many thought we did. They told my husband that he was worst than a unbeliever because he wasn't working at a nine to five job. They said I didn't want my husband to work because I was too insecure to have him out of my presence. They said we were both lazy freeloaders that did not want to work and only wanted handouts. We hated asking anyone for anything, so that's definitely a lie! When we didn't ask and would just rather go without instead, they said we were prideful. They just wanted updates on our struggle so they could feel good about where they were in life. These people were really trying to make us mentally crazy. I'm just thankful that we had our own relationship with God and could hear Him for ourselves. A personal relationship with God is so important! God chose our process, so in the wilderness we went with limited resources kicking and screaming every day.

Even those that said they would help with my installment service backed out once they heard we were homeless sleeping in the car. All they had to do was show up as support! That's it! We didn't ask for much, just their time so we didn't feel alone that day. Days prior to them getting the information that we were homeless, they all said God assigned them to help us with my installment because it was God's will. Then soon as they heard we were homeless, they all said we were out of God's Will and they did not want to support us because they didn't want their names attached to anything in case other people found out. So one minute we were in God's Will, but the next minute we were not??? People really switched up on us like it was nothing. Thankfully God just continued to show us people's true colors and motives. This warfare was like nothing I would've ever imagined. I was already emotional and crying out to God every day telling Him I wanted the service to be postponed. I just wasn't up for it anymore now that we were going through lose and a test. I was no longer happy or excited about the installment service. I thought it was suppose to be a celebration, but it just looked like chaos of a storm. When all the women for my installment backed out, I thought that was my answer from God to postpone the service, but it wasn't. It was just another test to see if we were going to remain dedicated to what God called us to do.

God told us we were not released from the date He gave us and we must go on without them. God wanted my husband/pastor to install me himself, not them. My husband/pastor was nervous as ever because he had never done an installment service before, but he knew God was leading him to step up to gain the experience. He had only been pastoring for a year and a half and I was not raised in the church, so we did not know anything about the procedure. The only installment service I've ever witnessed was my husband's and at that time I did not even know him. We both were nervous and scared, but did not want to disobey God in any way! We were scared that if we didn't follow through, it would prolong our homeless process.

On July 15th 2018, we woke up from sleeping in the car in a supermarket parking lot, we took turns going to the supermarket bathroom to freshen up, and got dressed for the big day. Installment day had finally arrived! I was feeling so many emotions that I just wanted to go back to sleep. I was pregnant with swollen feet that could barely fit in my shoes and let's not talk about clothing. I felt so dirty because we had not taken a real shower in weeks!! I just didn't have that much push left in me, but I knew I had to keep moving forward with tears and all. If I never knew God was real before, I knew He was real in my life now. He kept our minds from going insane and kept our health in tact. Although we still felt a little discouraged, we drove to the designated church that would allow us to rent it for two hours with no gas nor money, but we made it!

We had to pay the church $150 for the two hours we needed it for, but did not have it. We didn't even have anyone to borrow it from either. As we pulled up to the door, I did not want to even go in because we couldn't pay for the rented time, nor did we know where it was coming from. God said to continue on, so we did! I didn't even think anyone would show up, not that I really cared at this point, but at least if people showed up they could sow so we could have something for the church rental fee! I prayed as I walk to the doors of the church and asked God to provide. He just said, "trust Him." Nervous about everything, I took the baby and just sat in the front row. A row I hated sitting in and would avoid at all costs, but it was my day to sit in the front row for all to see. I figured it wasn't so bad this time because no one would be there, until it was! People started walking through the door as my husband/pastor set up a couple things and I was surprised at all the faces that showed up. People

I would have never guessed walked through the doors. I had to fight back tears! All those that I thought would attend, did not. All those that I thought would not attend, did! It was okay because God was just continuing to show me my supporters. I was grateful for all of them. We went on with the service and ended up raising $200! We had enough to pay the church and something for the drummer and the one who played the keyboard for the service. I was relieved not only because it was over and we got through it, but we were able to pay our debt to the church. By the way, God definitely had His way in the service and I could not have asked for anything different. If it wasn't God's Will, I'm sure He would've never been present. But the fact that He was there, gave us all the more comfort.

Back to the car we went with very little gas, praying all the way to find a safe place so we could park and sleep. We received a call that night from someone who wanted to sow a few dollars into our ministry and we just thanked God because we were able to put it towards gas. We slept in the car for another couple of weeks until God told us to attend a church service of an old acquaintance of my husband's. I was not in the mood to go to any church, or anywhere for that matter. I was drained emotionally, mentally, and physically. I knew if God said to go it was for a reason, so I sat aside my feelings and we went. The service was nice. It helped us to take our minds off of the fact we were sleeping in the car! At the end of the service, one of the ministry leaders pulled us to the side and asks us how we were doing. She wanted to know what was going on as if she knew something was strange already. My husband felt comfortable enough to tell her a small piece of our situation, then she immediately told us that we were out of God's Will for our life because God would not have us in the car like that. I thought to myself, here we go again with Job's friends! God can do anything He want to do with whoever He wants to do it to! So we have to stop putting limits on God. Again, of course we didn't sign up for this. We were considered without our consent! I tuned her out of my head and was ready to go at that point, but God had me to wait a little longer.

Although she too spoke just as Job's friends did, God pushed her to help us. She connected us to a man that owned a rooming house and she paid for two weeks so we could stay there. We were grateful to get out of the car and to be able to take a real shower, cook hot food, and to stretch out! When we arrived at the house it looked like a dump and we felt like we were in prison because of the bars on all of the windows. There were even crackheads living inside the house and there was a lot of traffic in and out of the house all day and night long. We were afraid to have our child there, but was still happy to be out of the car for a little time. We definitely would've went back to the car if we needed to and we already made up in our minds that after the two weeks were over, we were out of there. This house was worse than the first house we had to stay in and we thought it could not get any worse than that! We were wrong! I had to ask God to show us that we were still in His Will after seeing that place because after looking around, doubt started to creep in again.

God deals with me using pennies when I feel unsure of something or somewhere. A penny would appear when I'm on the right track or in the right place. Just as I began to cry, I looked over out the window and noticed pennies were lined up on the window ledge. I checked the room from top to bottom when we first got there and I was certain they were not there before, so I knew it was God's purpose for us to be even there. We didn't know why, but we had to trust Him all the way. I wiped my eyes and continued with the process. Process was turned up 7 times greater now that I was a pastor too, but we did not have to sleep in the car for now (praise God). After the two weeks were up, God had us to shift from one stranger's house to the next in very short intervals to stay. It was like death because we would've never imagined this for our lives! We were ready to give up every day, but something inside of us (Holy Spirit) would not allow us to do so. I was over living in persecution, lack, and poverty for the sake of following Jesus, but we had to keep pressing! Don't get me wrong, I love God, but I was tired of process!!! We brought our oldest two kids back to stay with us because I just could not be away from them any longer. Stranger's house or not, I just felt the pull to have them close again.

All of the strangers that we lived with were ministry leaders so we thought they will help the process be a little smoother, wrong! They had drama on top of drama and some were witches and warlocks (preying on others, rebellious, disobedient, and etc...) in the spiritual realm, but were disguised as holy men and women of God to the people with no discernment. God was showing me what not to do in ministry and that He was not pleased with these people! Everything and everyone was not only part of the process, but it was training for me as well. Pastors, as well as other leaders that God chose, have a standard to uphold. We can not live just any type of way! They say you never know how a person really is until you live with them, and boy were they right! I didn't want to see anymore. I just wanted to shut my eyes and pray that time would pass by so that everything would be over, but there was still more to the process! The expectation of a ministry leader is heavy and we are held to a higher standard by God, but with God all things are possible to accomplish.

> "Here is a trustworthy saying: Whoever aspires to be an overseer desires a noble task. Now the overseer is to be above reproach, faithful to his wife, temperate, self-controlled, respectable, hospitable, able to teach, not given to drunkenness, not violent but gentle, not quarrelsome, not a lover of money. He must manage his own family well and see that his children obey him, and he must do so in a manner worthy of full respect. (If anyone does not know how to manage his own family, how can he take care of God's church?) He must not be a recent convert, or he may become conceited and fall under the same judgment as the devil. He must also have a good reputation with outsiders, so that he will not fall into disgrace and into the devil's trap."
> 1 Timothy 3:1-7 NIV

I received so much backlash now that I had become a pastor. I had people saying women had no right to preach because they were to sit and be quiet. People said I shouldn't be allowed to preach because I didn't speak in tongues. They imply that I wasn't filled with the Holy Spirit because my tongues was not evident to them. Let me kill this demon of religion right now! Once you accept Salvation and allow Jesus Christ into your heart, He automatically fills you with His spirit (The Holy Spirit). Yes, tongues is the evidence for "Others" to know you are filled with Him, but as long as YOU know you accepted Jesus, you were filled even if tongues have not been released out of you just yet. What are tongues? Tongues is a gift from God and He gives them to anyone who is open and willing to accept them. God also has His own timing in releasing them unto you, so don't stress listening to the people. Just be patient. Tongues are a heavenly language that only God can understand and they strengthen you spiritually.

> *"For anyone who speaks in a tongue does not speak to people but to God. Indeed, no one understands them; they utter mysteries by the Spirit."*
> *1 Corinthians 14:2 NIV*

> *"Anyone who speaks in a tongue edifies themselves, but the one who prophesies edifies the church. I would like every one of you to speak in tongues, but I would rather have you prophesy. The one who prophesies is greater than the one who speaks in tongues, unless someone interprets, so that the church may be edified."*
> *1 Corinthians 14:4-5 NIV*

Others told me I was trying to take my husband's spotlight instead of letting him do all the preaching! Their plan was to turn my husband and I against each other so we didn't work together in ministry. They wanted us to think we had to compete against one another. Satan knew we were a major force to deal with when working together, so he used whoever he could. Some said I was released prematurely and I was not built for the warfare or office of a pastor. I had to endure all of these irrelevant people saying all of these untrue things to me and about me, all while remaining humble and quiet! I wanted to shoot them all one bullet to the head, as my professor would say. They definitely died a few times in my head, but God insured me that He knew all and seen all. I just needed to relax. He knew they were disrespecting the anointing on my life, but He had to remind me that it wasn't about me. It was the people disrespecting GOD on the inside of me, not me personally! They disrespected His son, Jesus, so why wouldn't they do the same to me if I was walking in Jesus's footsteps?? It was something to think about. I didn't like any of it, but it was all part of my process! My process just made me respect Jesus Christ all the more. He went through process for us and continued all the way until the very end. Me on the other hand, I wanted to run away every single day! I continued on because I loved God enough to obey.

People don't tell you all the details of walking with God. They always portray it as skipping with smiles, pretty flowers, and sliding down colorful rainbows, but it's actually sacrifice and nothing comes cheap or for free! Sacrifice is truly death! While everyone was either jealous, envious, or hated what they saw in me, they had no idea what I faced behind the scenes or even in front of the scenes! The warfare. The rage. The anger. The resentment. The doubt. The hurt and pain. The loss. The stress. The rejection. The lies. The persecution. The scandals. The suffering! I knew for a fact that any of them that wanted my place could not walk in my shoes for a moment without losing their mind, but they wanted to be me so bad though. I never understood this way of thinking and maybe it wasn't for me to understand.

Many nights I cried myself to sleep wondering if Jesus did the same. I felt rejection from every side. I did not understand all that God was doing and it had my mind all over the place. I began to worry myself so much everyday that I could barely sleep!! God was pulling me closer and closer to Him. Yes, I wanted to be close to God, but not at this expense. Jesus! I had multiple processes happening at one time, but did not realize it until God revealed why the fire was so intense! I had process as a believer of Jesus Christ, process as a wife, process as a Godly mother shaping our children into who God called them to be, process as a pastor, and process for the people I was going to lead! I couldn't believe we were being hit with so many chapters of life struggles at once, but honestly without God I would have died a long time ago! This walk with God is very challenging, but I would rather do it with Him than without Him. Life before Him, I was on the verge of taking my own life everyday, but God came in and set me free from all of that. He healed me. He restored me. He delivered me. He loves on me daily. He took me in as His own. Once I accepted Him, He kept my mind from going crazy and kept me protected. This walk with God is actually worth it, but the reprogramming of my mind and how I thought life would be was a task all by itself.

Chapter 8

God was building my character. According to the world, I thought I was a model citizen. God showed me differently. His word say, "be not conformed to this world, but be transformed by the renewing of your mind." I had to allow God to renew my mind. He showed me my flaws and they were ugly. I thought I had buried those things, but God wanted them to be uprooted and burned. I had to allow the process before God could move. God is a gentleman and He doesn't force anything on us. We have a choice to follow Him or to stay stuck in our own ways. It definitely isn't a good ideal to stay stuck in our own ways because that's where Satan could snatch us up!

God had to get me to a place where I shared His heart again for the people He entrusted me to lead them. Don't get me wrong, I love people, but I do not accept no mess from them! I've been hurt many times in the past and my process only brought on more hurt. I had to get back to a place that I trusted people again. God began healing all the bruises and scars I got from the people which was the first step. If was don't trust someone, then we can not love them with the love of God because God's love states love always trust. I even had to practice forgiveness until it became natural and easy for me. We have to forgive one another in order for God to forgive us. I know I haven't mastered being perfect, so I need God to forgive me everyday! This process hurt, but I knew it was all for the best.

I trusted God with all of me, so in process I had to walk in humility and gratefulness every step of the way. The *"Beatitudes"* is the posture our hearts should be in everyday.

> *"and Jesus began to teach them. He said:*
> *"Blessed are the poor in spirit, for theirs is the kingdom of heaven.*
> *Blessed are those who mourn, for they will be comforted.*
> *Blessed are the meek, for they will inherit the earth.*
> *Blessed are those who hunger and thirst for righteousness, for they will be filled.*
> *Blessed are the merciful, for they will be shown mercy.*
> *Blessed are the pure in heart, for they will see God.*
> *Blessed are the peacemakers, for they will be called children of God.*
> *Blessed are those who are persecuted because of righteousness, for theirs is the kingdom of heaven.*
> *Blessed are you when people insult you, persecute you and falsely say all kinds of evil against you because of me. Rejoice and be glad, because great is your reward in heaven, for in the same way they persecuted the prophets who were before you."*
> *Matthew 5:2-12 NIV*

Character matters a lot to God because we all suppose to resemble Him and He doesn't want to be portrayed incorrectly. I understood this more and more each day. It was a lot to take in. God have an image, and He wants to see it through us. God created us in His image and He do not want to see anything else. When I accepted Salvation, I did not realize that a daily growth inside of us all had to take place! It doesn't stop at just accepting Jesus Christ into your life. God was maturing me and wanting it done fast because of where He was taking me. He did not want me to stay stagnant or spiritually immature. I've seen some stagnant people and it was sad to watch actually. I had to grow and

He made sure of it.

I would remember sitting in different services and hearing the preacher say we should all be fruit inspectors. I always wondered exactly what that meant? God surely let me in on what it meant and I was sorry I asked... just kidding. God was showing me the fruits of the spirit. Fruits of what spirit? The Holy Spirit that is! God wanted me to possess the fruits of The Holy Spirit and He did not want anything less. I had some fruits, but He wanted me to possess them all and He wanted them fully matured on the inside of me. What are the fruits?

-Love

-Joy

-Peace

-Patience

-Kindness

-Goodness

-Faithfulness

-Gentleness

-Self-Control

"But the fruit of the Spirit is love, joy, peace, forbearance, kindness, goodness, faithfulness, gentleness and self-control. Against such things there is no law."
Galatians 5:22-23 NIV

These were the characteristics that I had to become and release to everyone. When I say everyone, I mean everyone even if they hurt me, talked about me, or used me. I had to always display all of these characteristics. It was definitely a process for me that I want to hurry through. It hurt to be stretched into maturity and purpose! I was one to hold grudges and to remember what "they" done to me. I wanted to seek revenge on all those who hurt me. I would keep a mental list of all those people and would hope that one day what I seen in my mind would come to pass. It was definitely nothing nice! Most of the time it would be me beating them until they couldn't get back up or they would just completely dropped dead altogether with just one blink of my eye. I knew this was one of the ugly parts of me that God was dealing with as well. I could not walk in the fruits of the spirit with this mindset. I had to let it go even if "they" were not sorry or never even apologized. This was hard for me, but I wanted to please God, so I followed the steps of process. Through all of this process, I still could not understand why God wanted to use me. I had so much going on with me that at one point I thought I wasn't able to be cleaned. Then I had to realize God is God and He can do all things, including cleaning me up and using me. God uses who He wants to use. If God can use a donkey to speak, then why wouldn't He be able to use me? God has all power to do the unthinkable, so we should just stop thinking and do whatever God tells us.

> "For my thoughts are not your thoughts, neither are your ways my ways," declares the Lord."
> Isaiah 55:8 NIV

We put God in a box and limit Him to what He can do because we can't wrap our minds around Him. Our minds are too small to measure God's ability. If we look throughout scripture God always use the unlikely. He did not go for the smart know-it-alls, or the high and mighty. He went for the humble and the willing. God just need us to yield to His Will and His ways, then

He could use us for anything and anywhere. I understood that God's way for my life was better, despite the process because I had tried it my way for so many years and failed each and every time! I needed God in my life to show me the way. Without Him I would be back in darkness not being able to see anything clearly. I had no problem yielding to God's Will, but the process was almost unexplainable. I know the only way I got through was because God was with me every step of the way. He never left me, and He always held me up when I was down and out. He carried me when I couldn't even stand for myself. He shielded me from so much harm that could've come my way. My life really could've went a lot worse, but God blocked it! I could've even died years prior, but God made sure that didn't happen. He wanted the purpose on my life to be fulfilled, no matter what because the price on my head was of great value to Him.

This next part of my process involved self-control, faithfulness, and transition, a major transition at that! My family and I had to relocate far, far away from our hometown. God wanted to protect what He was doing in and through us, so He told my husband and I to pack up our children and leave behind everything and everybody. We had to go to a foreign land where we knew no one! God had us all in a start over season where everything had to be new. We were connected to contaminated people, places, and things that had us bound. We were stuck running in small circles not being able to move forward no matter what we did!! God revealed to us that the very ones we thought were suppose to help us, was only hindering us. We had to disconnect completely because our lives, marriage, family, ministry, and businesses depended on it! I didn't have a problem with leaving that very moment, but my husband still had concerns. We truly had nothing holding us in Pennsylvania or New Jersey because we were homeless, no jobs, no vehicle, no money, and no genuine support! We were bouncing from one stranger's home to the next at this point, our truck that we recently purchased had gotten taken away because we couldn't keep up with the registration and insurance fees, no job would hire us, and all savings were gone! I'm sure God had it to happen that way so we would move in His timing and not ours or the peoples. We knew if God said it, He would make a way and He did.

We gathered up our now four children and awaited God's instructions. God gave us detailed instructions on exactly where to go and how the way would be made. We did nothing on our own! We had one suitcase that held a few outfits for each of us and a small bag with formula, wipes, and diapers for our newborn. Everything else we left behind and we had just enough money to make it where we were going. We did not know what was in store for us in this new place, but we had to go. We arrived by bus and it felt like it was the longest trip in history!!!! Everything was different and took some getting used to. We was not fully out of the process just yet, but it definitely calmed down a lot. We still had to spiritually fight and stay on the wall of prayer. We were still moving from one stranger's house to the next, but at a higher speed! At this rate we knew we would be in our own place in no time! We trusted God through it all, even though we were all afraid. A month and a couple weeks into the new land, we got our own place through the grace of God!! We knew it was nothing but God because we had no job and no money! God gave us favor with the owner. We were so grateful and relieved to be living in our own place again!!!! We did not have to put up with other people, their stupid made up rules, manipulation, lies, or control any longer! We finally felt FREE again. It took 100% Faith in God and blocking out any other voice that went against God's Will for our life! Many had so much to say and they are still talking from the same place we left them in. We know God have so much in store for us and our new place was only a glimpse of what He has waiting.

Chapter 9

In this new place I had a chance to grow spiritually, be free, and step into my calling as a pastor on a greater level. I never thought I could do it, but with God anything is possible. It took some getting used to, but I took the chance and was happy I did. God touched so many lives through me in a short period of time, and I know He is not through with me yet. I'm just honored He chose me, no matter how much I ran or what people thought I wasn't worthy of the calling. Every day is a process for me, but that's okay because it shows me that God is still with me. In fact, in this new land God is rewriting my story. I'm sure in due time milk and honey will be my portion everywhere I turn. Why? Because God said it and I am believing Him for it every day.

I also plan to continue growing as a pastor. A pastor, elder, overseer, bishop, or priest pretty much is all the same thing. They each just have a couple of details in their job description that are different. Just what is a pastor according to the scriptures?

"An elder must be blameless, faithful to his wife, a man whose children believe and are not open to the charge of being wild and disobedient. Since an overseer manages God's household, he must be blameless—not overbearing, not quick-tempered, not given to drunkenness, not violent, not pursuing dishonest gain. Rather, he must be hospitable,

one who loves what is good, who is self-controlled, upright, holy and disciplined. He must hold firmly to the trustworthy message as it has been taught, so that he can encourage others by sound doctrine and refute those who oppose it."
Titus 1:6-9 NIV

I know you are reading this scripture and thinking like most with a few questions. Main question I know your asking is, how can a woman be a pastor if the scripture is referring to a man? Good question, because I asked the same thing. After some research and spending some time in prayer with the Holy Spirit, I realized times were different back then compared to now. God is the same God yesterday, today, and forever, but He will do new things to get our attention. In the book of Isaiah, God wants us to realize He does new things that seem impossible or crazy to us. Back then women were not allowed to speak, so God used that and turned it around for our good. Now women are able to speak for the glory of God. Here are two scriptures that are similar which proves just that.

"In the last days, God says, I will pour out my Spirit on all people. Your sons and daughters will prophesy, your young men will see visions, your old men will dream dreams. Even on my servants, both men and women, I will pour out my Spirit in those days, and they will prophesy."
Acts 2:17-18 NIV

"And afterward, I will pour out my Spirit on all people. Your sons and daughters will prophesy, your old men will dream dreams, your young men will see visions. Even on my servants, both men and women, I will pour out my Spirit in those days."
Joel 2:28-29 NIV

These scriptures are letting us know that in the last days God will use all people, male and female. We are definitely in the last days according to scripture. God is sending out the least likely and there is nothing anyone can do about it. The least likely have been kicked down and talked about for so long that being low is their posture. They understand that being low is what it means to be humble. God trust and choose those who are humble and grateful. Now I'm not saying men are not humble, because there are still some great men of God that are still humble and willing to do the work of The Lord at any cost. My husband is definitely one of them, so I'm not bashing the men. I'm just making it clear that women are making their way to the forefront with the shift of God. Women are more than capable to submit to God and deliver His message. So yes, women can be pastors, why? Because God can do whatever He wants to do. Period! God made me a pastor, no one else. When you are a pastor, you have to walk in God's love no matter what to be effective. What is God's love?

> *"Love is patient, love is kind. It does not envy, it does not boast, it is not proud. It does not dishonor others, it is not self-seeking, it is not easily angered, it keeps no record of wrongs. Love does not delight in evil but rejoices with the truth. It always protects, always trusts, always hopes, always perseveres. Love never fails."*
> *1 Corinthians 13:4-8 NIV*

It is important to walk in God's love and not the world's love. The world's love is selfish and wicked. Pastors have to have a pure heart and clean hands, so they have to live a life of repentance. What does it mean to repent? To feel regret about one's wrongdoings and want to change.

> *"Repent, then, and turn to God, so that your sins may be wiped out, that times of refreshing may come from the Lord,"*
> *Acts 3:19 NIV*

Lastly, it is important to always forgive. Forgiveness is not for the other person, it is for you. We lock ourselves in prison and block God out when we don't forgive. God wants to always move in our lives, but He won't when we don't forgive. Holding grudges stops us from getting blessed by God. I don't know about you, but I can't afford God closing His hands on me. Being a pastor speaking the pure gospel, will bring hurt, lies upon your name, and persecution. There will always be someone to punch in the face, but us as pastors have to turn the other cheek and forgive. God will seek justice and vengeance on our behalf. So allow God to be God, because He has the power to do anything!

> *"Bear with each other and forgive one another if any of you has a grievance against someone. Forgive as the Lord forgave you."*
> *Colossians 3:13 NIV*

Being a pastor is hard work and should not be taken lightly. We are held to a higher standard, so God requires more of us.

"Not many of you should become teachers, my fellow believers, because you know that we who teach will be judged more strictly."
James 3:1 NIV

"Do your best to present yourself to God as one approved, a worker who does not need to be ashamed and who correctly handles the word of truth."
2 Timothy 2:15 NIV

> *"When we direct the affairs of the church well, we are worthy of double honor."*
> 1 Timothy 5:17

Overall, being a pastor is an important job and I knew that from the beginning. I just don't think I realized how much warfare came with the title. I've faced so many things that I didn't think was possible! I've had miscarriages due to witchcraft performed on me. Warlocks wanted me dead. People right in the church prayed my husband and I divorced so they could devour him. People that professed to love God, hated our children and tried to divide our family. Our own relatives turned their backs on us and even turned against us. The very ones that I thought were there to support, mentor, and push my family and I to the next level, set out to hinder and destroy us because they could see where God was taking us and they were not going to gain anything in return. I went through a wilderness period along with my family of course, just as Yeshua/Jesus did. Even God ordains test to occur to see how strong in faith we are. I love the fact that God showed us even His very own son went through test just as we still do today. It is God's Will for us to go through things that does not feel good or make sense. Don't take my word for it. Please read it for yourself:

"Then Jesus was led by the Spirit into the wilderness to be tempted by the devil. After fasting forty days and forty nights, he was hungry. The tempter came to him and said, "If you are the Son of God, tell these stones to become bread." Jesus answered, "It is written: 'Man shall not live on bread alone, but on every word that comes from the mouth of God.'" Then the devil took him to the holy city and had him stand on the highest point of the temple. "If you are the Son of God," he said, "throw yourself down. For it is written: "'He will command his angels

concerning you, and they will lift you up in their hands, so that you will not strike your foot against a stone.' " Jesus answered him, "It is also written: 'Do not put the Lord your God to the test.' " Again, the devil took him to a very high mountain and showed him all the kingdoms of the world and their splendor. "All this I will give you," he said, "if you will bow down and worship me." Jesus said to him, "Away from me, Satan! For it is written: 'Worship the Lord your God, and serve him only.' " Then the devil left him, and angels came and attended him."
Matthew 4:1-11 NIV

I know at some point you must have asked yourself did I overcome and if so, how? Remember, I said anything is possible with God! As long as we allow God to lead us, we can overcome anything! We must also stand firm on God's Word so that the enemy will flee. I pray my testimony helps you to overcome whatever stands in your way. Just know you are stronger than you think.

"You, dear children, are from God and have overcome them, because the one who is in you is greater than the one who is in the world."
1 John 4:4 NIV

"They triumphed over him by the blood of the Lamb and by the word of their testimony; they did not love their lives so much as to shrink from death."
Revelation 12:11 NIV

The blood of the Lamb is the blood Yeshua/Jesus shedded for us because He is the Lamb that was sacrificed for us! Yeshua/Jesus went through death, burial, and resurrection, so I could live. He died for me. He died for you. I was able to overcome because of Him.

These two songs below helped me to get through when I wanted to give up. I had to fall into a place a worship with God. Maybe these two songs will help you too!

- Steffany Gretzinger, *"Reckless Love."*

- Anthony Brown & Group Therapy, *"Worth."*

As a pastor or leader of God's ministry, we can not allow warfare, people, places, or things to get in the way of our job description. Our heart posture have to be right before God. We have to lead the sheep "God's people" with compassion and understanding. We are to be disciples of Yeshua/Jesus Christ and He led with love and kindness. Yeshua/Jesus didn't step out of character, although I'm sure He wanted to a number of times. People did a lot of wrong to Yeshua/Jesus, but He still stayed true to His assignment. Yeshua/Jesus has shown us the way and the truth, therefore we have life through Him. We now have to lead others to Yeshua/Jesus so they too can learn the truth and have eternal life. We have to stop leading people to ourselves and/or the church building. Only Yeshua/Jesus have the power to save a soul and provide everlasting life. If we do not lead others to Yeshua/Jesus they will not have life and will continue to wander in darkness. We are nothing without Yeshua/Jesus no matter what title or position we hold! Again, I say lead others to Yeshua/Jesus. After the lost gain an understanding of Yeshua/Jesus, then you can lead them to a church building that trains and equips individuals with an understanding of God's Word. One plants the seed, another waters the seed, and God grows the increase!

www.ingramcontent.com/pod-product-compliance
Lightning Source LLC
Chambersburg PA
CBHW071320080526
44587CB00018B/3294